Bipolar:

Questions and Answers

Causes, Symptoms, Signs, Diagnosis and Treatments

National Institute of Mental Health (Author), National Institutes of Health (Author), US Department of Health and Human Services (Author), S.Smith (Editor), S. Smith (Illustrator)

BIPOLAR DISORDER

Table of Contents

Introduction: Bipolar Disorder

This booklet discusses bipolar disorder in adults. For information on bipolar disorder in children and adolescents, see the NIMH booklet, "Bipolar Disorder in Children and Teens: A Parent's Guide."

Bipolar Disorder

What is bipolar disorder?

Bipolar

Bipolar disorder, also known as manic-depressive illness, is a brain disorder that causes unusual shifts in mood, energy, activity levels, and the ability to carry out day-to-day tasks. Symptoms of bipolar disorder are severe. They are different from the normal ups and downs that everyone goes through from time to time. Bipolar disorder symptoms can result in damaged relationships, poor job or school performance, and even suicide. But bipolar disorder can be treated, and people with this illness can lead full and productive lives.

Bipolar disorder often develops in a person's late teens or early adult years. At least half of all cases start before age 25.1

Some people have their first symptoms during childhood, while others may develop symptoms late in life.

Bipolar disorder is not easy to spot when it starts. The symptoms may seem like separate problems, not recognized as parts of a larger problem. Some people suffer for years before they are properly diagnosed and treated. Like diabetes or heart disease, bipolar disorder is a long-term illness that must be carefully managed throughout a person's life.

What are the symptoms of bipolar disorder?

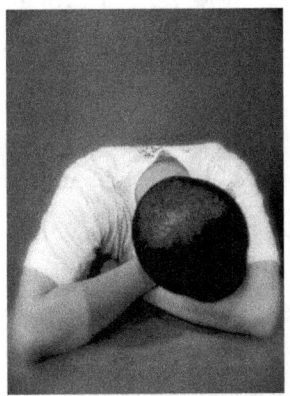

People with bipolar disorder experience unusually intense emotional states that occur in distinct periods called "mood episodes." An overly joyful or overexcited state is called a manic episode, and an extremely sad or hopeless state is called a depressive episode. Sometimes, a mood episode includes symptoms of both mania and depression. This is called a mixed state. People with bipolar disorder also may be explosive and irritable during a mood episode.

Extreme changes in energy, activity, sleep, and behavior go along with these changes in mood. It is possible for someone with bipolar disorder to experience a long-lasting period of unstable moods rather than discrete episodes of depression or mania.

Bipolar Disorder

A person may be having an episode of bipolar disorder if he or she has a number of manic or depressive symptoms for most of the day, nearly every day, for at least one or two weeks. Sometimes symptoms are so severe that the person cannot function normally at work, school, or home.

Symptoms of bipolar disorder are described below. Symptoms of mania or a manic episode include:

Mood Changes

- A long period of feeling "high," or an overly happy or outgoing mood

- Extremely irritable mood, agitation, feeling "jumpy" or "wired."

Behavioral Changes

- Talking very fast, jumping from one idea to another, having racing thoughts
- Being easily distracted
- Increasing goal-directed activities, such as taking on new projects
- Being restless
- Sleeping little

What are the symptoms of bipolar disorder?

- Having an unrealistic belief in one's abilities
- Behaving impulsively and taking part in a lot of pleasurable,
- high-risk behaviors, such as spending sprees, impulsive sex, and impulsive business investments.

Symptoms of depression or a depressive episode include:

Mood Changes

- A long period of feeling worried or empty

- Loss of interest in activities once enjoyed, including sex.

Behavioral Changes

- Feeling tired or "slowed down"
- Having problems concentrating, remembering, and making decisions
- Being restless or irritable
- Changing eating, sleeping, or other habits
- Thinking of death or suicide, or attempting suicide.

Bipolar Disorder

In addition to mania and depression, bipolar disorder can cause a range of moods, as shown on the scale.

One side of the scale includes severe depression, moderate depression, and mild low mood. Moderate depression may cause less extreme symptoms, and mild low mood is called dysthymia when it is chronic or long-term. In the middle of the scale is normal or balanced mood.

At the other end of the scale are hypomania and severe mania. Some people with bipolar disorder experience hypomania. During hypomanic episodes, a person may have increased energy and activity levels that are not as severe as typical mania, or he or she may have episodes that last less than a week and do not require emergency care. A person having a hypomanic episode may feel very good, be highly productive, and function well. This person may not feel that anything is wrong even as family and friends recognize the mood swings as possible bipolar disorder. Without proper treatment, however, people with hypomania may develop severe mania or depression.

During a mixed state, symptoms often include agitation, trouble sleeping, major changes in appetite, and suicidal thinking. People in a mixed state may feel very sad or hopeless while feeling extremely energized.

What are the symptoms of bipolar disorder?

Sometimes, a person with severe episodes of mania or depression has psychotic symptoms too, such as hallucinations or delusions. The psychotic symptoms tend to reflect the person's extreme mood. For example, psychotic symptoms for a person having a manic episode may include believing he or she is famous, has a lot of money, or has special powers. In the same way, a person having a depressive episode may believe he or she is ruined and penniless, or has committed a crime. As a result, people with bipolar disorder who have psychotic symptoms are sometimes wrongly diagnosed as having schizophrenia, another severe mental illness that is linked with hallucinations and delusions.

People with bipolar disorder may also have behavioral problems. They may abuse alcohol or substances, have relationship problems, or perform poorly in school or at work. At first, it's not easy to recognize these problems as signs of a major mental illness.

How does bipolar disorder affect someone over time?

Bipolar disorder usually lasts a lifetime. Episodes of mania and depression typically come back over time. Between episodes, many people with bipolar disorder are free of symptoms, but some people may have lingering symptoms.

Doctors usually diagnose mental disorders using guidelines from the Diagnostic and Statistical Manual of Mental Disorders, or DSM. According to the DSM, there are four basic types of bipolar disorder:

1. Bipolar I Disorder is mainly defined by manic or mixed episodes that last at least seven days, or by manic symptoms that are so severe that the person needs immediate hospital care. Usually, the person also has depressive episodes, typically lasting at least two weeks. The symptoms of mania or depression must be a major change from the person's normal behavior.

2. Bipolar II Disorder is defined by a pattern of depressive episodes shifting back and forth with hypomanic episodes, but no full-blown manic or mixed episodes.

3. Bipolar Disorder Not Otherwise Specified (BP-NOS) is diagnosed when a person has symptoms of the illness that do not meet diagnostic criteria for either bipolar I or II. The symptoms may not last long enough, or the person may have too few symptoms, to be diagnosed with bipolar I or II. However, the symptoms are clearly out of the person's normal range of behavior.

4. Cyclothymic Disorder, or Cyclothymia, is a mild form of bipolar disorder. People who have cyclothymia have episodes of hypomania that shift back and forth with mild depression for at least two years. However, the symptoms do not meet the diagnostic requirements for any other type of bipolar disorder.

Some people may be diagnosed with rapid-cycling bipolar disorder. This is when a person has four or more episodes of major depression, mania, hypomania, or mixed symptoms within a year.2 Some people experience more than one episode in a week, or even within one day. Rapid cycling seems to be more common in people who have severe bipolar disorder and may be more common in people who have their first episode at a younger age. One study found that people with rapid cycling had their first episode about four years earlier, during mid to late teen years, than people without rapid cycling bipolar disorder.3 Rapid cycling affects more women than men.4

How does bipolar disorder affect someone over time?

Bipolar disorder tends to worsen if it is not treated. Over time, a person may suffer more frequent and more severe episodes than when the illness first appeared.5 Also, delays in getting the correct diagnosis and treatment make a person more likely to experience personal, social, and work-related problems.6

Proper diagnosis and treatment helps people with bipolar disorder lead healthy and productive lives. In most cases, treatment can help reduce the frequency and severity of episodes.

What illnesses often co-exist with bipolar disorder?

Substance abuse is very common among people with bipolar disorder, but the reasons for this link are unclear.7 Some people with bipolar disorder may try to treat their symptoms with alcohol or drugs. However, substance abuse may trigger or prolong bipolar symptoms, and the behavioral control problems associated with mania can result in a person drinking too much.

Anxiety disorders, such as post-traumatic stress disorder (PTSD) and social phobia, also co-occur often among people with bipolar disorder.8-10 Bipolar disorder also co-occurs with attention deficit hyperactivity disorder (ADHD), which has some symptoms that overlap with bipolar disorder, such as restlessness and being easily distracted.

People with bipolar disorder are also at higher risk for thyroid disease, migraine headaches, heart disease, diabetes, obesity, and other physical illnesses.10, 11 These illnesses may cause symptoms of mania or depression. They may also result from treatment for bipolar disorder.

Other illnesses can make it hard to diagnose and treat bipolar disorder. People with bipolar disorder should monitor their physical and mental health. If a symptom does not get better with treatment, they should tell their doctor.

What are the risk factors for bipolar disorder?

Scientists are learning about the possible causes of bipolar disorder. Most scientists agree that there is no single cause. Rather, many factors likely act together to produce the illness or increase risk.

Genetics

Bipolar disorder tends to run in families, so researchers are looking for genes that may increase a person's chance of developing the illness. Genes are the "building blocks" of heredity. They help control how the body and brain work and grow. Genes are contained inside a person's cells that are passed down from parents to children.

Children with a parent or sibling who has bipolar disorder are four to six times more likely to develop the illness, compared with children who do not have a family history of bipolar disorder.12 However, most children with a family history of bipolar disorder will not develop the illness.

Genetic research on bipolar disorder is being helped by advances in technology. This type of research is now much quicker and more far-reaching than in the past. One example is the launch of the Bipolar Disorder Phenome Database, funded in part by NIMH. Using the database, scientists will be able to link visible signs of the disorder with the genes that may influence them. So far, researchers using this database found that most people with bipolar disorder had:13

- Missed work because of their illness
- Other illnesses at the same time, especially alcohol and/or substance abuse and panic disorders
- Been treated or hospitalized for bipolar disorder.

The researchers also identified certain traits that appeared to run in families, including:

- History of psychiatric hospitalization
- Co-occurring obsessive-compulsive disorder (OCD)
- Age at first manic episode

What are the risk factors for bipolar disorder?

- Number and frequency of manic episodes.

Scientists continue to study these traits, which may help them find the genes that cause bipolar disorder some day.

But genes are not the only risk factor for bipolar disorder. Studies of identical twins have shown that the twin of a person with bipolar illness does not always develop the disorder. This is important because identical twins share all of the same genes. The study results suggest factors besides genes are also at work. Rather, it is likely that many different genes and a person's environment are involved. However, scientists do not yet fully understand how these factors interact to cause bipolar disorder.

Brain structure and functioning

Brain-imaging studies are helping scientists learn what happens in the brain of a person with bipolar disorder.14, 15 Newer brain-imaging tools, such as functional magnetic resonance imaging (fMRI) and positron emission tomography (PET), allow researchers to take pictures of the living brain at work. These tools help scientists study the brain's structure and activity.

Some imaging studies show how the brains of people with bipolar disorder may differ from the brains of healthy people or people with other mental disorders. For example, one study using MRI found that the pattern of brain development in children with bipolar disorder was similar to that in children with "multi-dimensional impairment," a disorder that causes symptoms that overlap somewhat with bipolar disorder and schizophrenia.16 This suggests that the common pattern of brain development may be linked to general risk for unstable moods.

Learning more about these differences, along with information gained from genetic studies, helps scientists better understand bipolar disorder. Someday scientists may be able to predict which types of treatment will work most effectively. They may even find ways to prevent bipolar disorder.

How is bipolar disorder diagnosed?

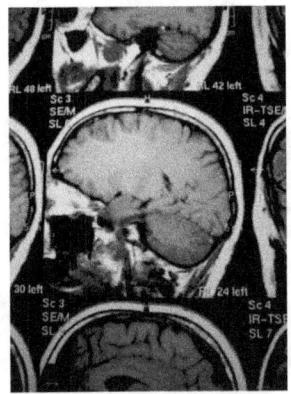

The first step in getting a proper diagnosis is to talk to a doctor, who may conduct a physical examination, an interview, and lab tests. Bipolar disorder cannot currently be identified through a blood test or a brain scan, but these tests can help rule out other contributing factors, such as a stroke or brain tumor. If the problems are not caused by other illnesses, the doctor may conduct a mental health evaluation. The doctor may also provide a referral to a trained mental health professional, such as a psychiatrist, who is experienced in diagnosing and treating bipolar disorder.

The doctor or mental health professional should conduct a complete diagnostic evaluation. He or she should discuss any family history of bipolar disorder or other mental illnesses and get a complete history of symptoms. The doctor or mental health professionals should also talk to the person's close relatives or spouse and note how they describe the person's symptoms and family medical history.

People with bipolar disorder are more likely to seek help when they are depressed than when experiencing mania or hypomania.17 Therefore, a careful medical history is needed to assure that bipolar disorder is not mistakenly diagnosed as major depressive disorder, which is also called unipolar depression. Unlike people with bipolar disorder, people who have unipolar depression do not experience mania. Whenever possible, previous records and input from family and friends should also be included in the medical history.

How is bipolar disorder treated?

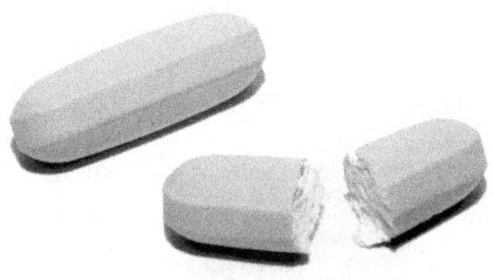

To date, there is no cure for bipolar disorder. But proper treatment helps most people with bipolar disorder gain better control of their mood swings and related symptoms.18-20 This is also true for people with the most severe forms of the illness.

Because bipolar disorder is a lifelong and recurrent illness, people with the disorder need long-term treatment to maintain control of bipolar symptoms. An effective maintenance treatment plan includes medication and psychotherapy for preventing relapse and reducing symptom severity.21

Medications

Bipolar disorder can be diagnosed and medications prescribed by people with an M.D. (doctor of medicine). Usually, bipolar medications are prescribed by a psychiatrist. In some states, clinical psychologists, psychiatric nurse practitioners, and advanced psychiatric nurse specialists can also prescribe medications. Check with your state's licensing agency to find out more.

Not everyone responds to medications in the same way. Several different medications may need to be tried before the best course of treatment is found.

Keeping a chart of daily mood symptoms, treatments, sleep patterns, and life events can help the doctor track and treat the illness most effectively. Sometimes this is called a daily life chart. If a person's symptoms change or if side effects become serious, the doctor may switch or add medications.

Some of the types of medications generally used to treat bipolar disorder are listed on the next page. Information on medications can change. For the most up to date information on use and side effects contact the U.S. Food and Drug Administration (FDA).

1. Mood stabilizing medications are usually the first choice to treat bipolar disorder. In general, people with bipolar disorder continue treatment with mood stabilizers for years. Except for lithium, many of these medications are anticonvul-

sants. Anticonvulsant medications are usually used to treat seizures, but they also help control moods. These medications are commonly used as mood stabilizers in bipolar disorder:

* Lithium (sometimes known as Eskalith or Lithobid) was the first mood-stabilizing medication approved by the U.S. Food and Drug Administration (FDA) in the 1970s for treatment of mania. It is often very effective in controlling symptoms of mania and preventing the recurrence of manic and depressive episodes.

* Valproic acid or divalproex sodium (Depakote), approved by the FDA in 1995 for treating mania, is a popular alternative to lithium for bipolar disorder. It is generally as effective as lithium for treating bipolar disorder.[23, 24] Also see the section in this booklet, "Should young women take valproic acid?"

* More recently, the anticonvulsant lamotrigine (Lamictal) received FDA approval for maintenance treatment of bipolar disorder.

* Other anticonvulsant medications, including gabapentin (Neurontin), topiramate (Topamax), and oxcarbazepine (Trileptal) are sometimes prescribed. No large studies have shown that these medications are more effective than mood stabilizers.

Valproic acid, lamotrigine, and other anticonvulsant medications have an FDA warning. The warning states that their use may increase the risk of suicidal thoughts and behaviors. People taking anticonvulsant medications for bipolar or other illnesses should be closely monitored for new or worsening symptoms of depression, suicidal thoughts or behavior, or any unusual changes in mood or behavior. People taking these medications should not make any changes without talking to their health care professional.

Lithium and Thyroid Function

People with bipolar disorder often have thyroid gland problems. Lithium treatment may also cause low thyroid levels in some people.22 Low thyroid function, called hypothyroidism, has been associated with rapid cycling in some people with bipolar disorder, especially women.

Because too much or too little thyroid hormone can lead to mood and energy changes, it is important to have a doctor check thyroid levels carefully. A person with bipolar disorder may need to take thyroid medication, in addition to medications for bipolar disorder, to keep thyroid levels balanced.

Should young women take valproic acid?

Valproic acid may increase levels of testosterone (a male hormone) in teenage girls and lead to polycystic ovary syndrome (PCOS) in women who begin taking the medication before age 20.25, 26 PCOS causes a woman's eggs to develop into cysts, or fluid filled sacs that collect in the ovaries instead of being released by monthly periods. This condition can cause obesity, excess body hair, disruptions in the menstrual cycle, and other serious symptoms. Most of these symptoms will improve after stopping treatment with valproic acid.27 Young girls and women taking valproic acid should be monitored carefully by a doctor.

2. Atypical antipsychotic medications are sometimes used to treat symptoms of bipolar disorder. Often, these medications are taken with other medications. Atypical antipsychotic medications are called "atypical" to set them apart from earlier medications, which are called "conventional" or "first-generation" antipsychotics.

* Olanzapine (Zyprexa), when given with an antidepressant medication, may help relieve symptoms of severe mania or psychosis.28 Olanzapine is also available in an injectable form, which quickly treats agitation associated with a manic or mixed episode. Olanzapine can be used for maintenance treatment of bipolar disorder as well, even when a person does not have

psychotic symptoms. However, some studies show that people taking olanzapine may gain weight and have other side effects that can increase their risk for diabetes and heart disease. These side effects are more likely in people taking olanzapine when compared with people prescribed other atypical antipsychotics.

* Aripiprazole (Abilify), like olanzapine, is approved for treatment of a manic or mixed episode. Aripiprazole is also used for maintenance treatment after a severe or sudden episode. As with olanzapine, aripiprazole also can be injected for urgent treatment of symptoms of manic or mixed episodes of bipolar disorder.

* Quetiapine (Seroquel) relieves the symptoms of severe and sudden manic episodes. In that way, quetiapine is like almost all antipsychotics. In 2006, it became the first atypical antipsychotic to also receive FDA approval for the treatment of bipolar depressive episodes.

* Risperidone (Risperdal) and ziprasidone (Geodon) are other atypical antipsychotics that may also be prescribed for controlling manic or mixed episodes.

3. Antidepressant medications are sometimes used to treat symptoms of depression in bipolar disorder. People with bipolar disorder who take antidepressants often take a mood stabilizer too. Doctors usually require this because taking only

an antidepressant can increase a person's risk of switching to mania or hypomania, or of developing rapid cycling symptoms.29 To prevent this switch, doctors who prescribe antidepressants for treating bipolar disorder also usually require the person to take a mood-stabilizing medication at the same time.

Recently, a large-scale, NIMH-funded study showed that for many people, adding an antidepressant to a mood stabilizer is no more effective in treating the depression than using only a mood stabilizer.30

* Fluoxetine (Prozac), paroxetine (Paxil), sertraline (Zoloft), and bupropion (Wellbutrin) are examples of antidepressants that may be prescribed to treat symptoms of bipolar depression.

Some medications are better at treating one type of bipolar symptoms than another. For example, lamotrigine (Lamictal) seems to be helpful in controlling depressive symptoms of bipolar disorder.

What are the side effects of these medications?

Before starting a new medication, people with bipolar disorder should talk to their doctor about the possible risks and benefits.

The psychiatrist prescribing the medication or pharmacist can also answer questions about side effects. Over the last decade, treatments have improved, and some medications now have fewer or more tolerable side effects than earlier treatments. However, everyone responds differently to medications. In some cases, side effects may not appear until a person has taken a medication for some time.

If the person with bipolar disorder develops any severe side effects from a medication, he or she should talk to the doctor who prescribed it as soon as possible. The doctor may change the dose or prescribe a different medication. People being treated for bipolar disorder should not stop taking a medication without talking to a doctor first. Suddenly stopping a medication may lead to "rebound," or worsening of bipolar disorder symptoms. Other uncomfortable or potentially dangerous withdrawal effects are also possible.

FDA Warning on Antidepressants

Antidepressants are safe and popular, but some studies have suggested that they may have unintentional effects on some people, especially in adolescents and young adults. The FDA warning says that patients of all ages taking antidepressants should be watched closely, especially during the first few weeks of treatment. Possible side effects to look for are depression that gets worse, suicidal thinking or behavior, or any unusual changes in behavior such as trouble sleeping, agitation, or withdrawal from normal social situations. Families and caregivers should report any changes to the doctor. For the latest information visit the FDA website.

The following sections describe some common side effects of the different types of medications used to treat bipolar disorder.

1. Mood Stabilizers

In some cases, lithium can cause side effects such as:

- Restlessness
- Dry mouth
- Bloating or indigestion
- Acne
- Unusual discomfort to cold temperatures
- Joint or muscle pain
- Brittle nails or hair.31

Lithium also causes side effects not listed here. If extremely bothersome or unusual side effects occur, tell your doctor as soon as possible.

If a person with bipolar disorder is being treated with lithium, it is important to make regular visits to the treating doctor. The doctor needs to check the levels of lithium in the person's blood, as well as kidney and thyroid function.

These medications may also be linked with rare but serious side effects. Talk with the treating doctor or a pharmacist to make sure you understand signs of serious side effects for the medications you're taking.

Common side effects of other mood stabilizing medications include:

- Drowsiness
- Dizziness
- Headache
- Diarrhea
- Constipation
- Heartburn
- Mood swings
- Stuffed or runny nose, or other cold-like symptoms.32-37

2. Atypical Antipsychotics

Some people have side effects when they start taking atypical antipsychotics. Most side effects go away after a few days and often can be managed successfully. People who are taking antipsychotics should not drive until they adjust to their new medication. Side effects of many antipsychotics include:

- Drowsiness
- Dizziness when changing positions
- Blurred vision
- Rapid heartbeat
- Sensitivity to the sun
- Skin rashes
- Menstrual problems for women.

Atypical antipsychotic medications can cause major weight gain and changes in a person's metabolism. This may increase a person's risk of getting diabetes and high cholesterol.38 A person's weight, glucose levels, and lipid levels should be monitored regularly by a doctor while taking these medications.

In rare cases, long-term use of atypical antipsychotic drugs may lead to a condition called tardive dyskinesia (TD). The condition causes muscle movements that commonly occur around the mouth. A person with TD cannot control these moments. TD can range from mild to severe, and it cannot always be cured. Some people with TD recover partially or fully after they stop taking the drug.

3. Antidepressants

The antidepressants most commonly prescribed for treating symptoms of bipolar disorder can also cause mild side effects that usually do not last long. These can include:

- Headache, which usually goes away within a few days.

- Nausea (feeling sick to your stomach), which usually goes away within a few days.

- Sleep problems, such as sleeplessness or drowsiness. This may happen during the first few weeks but then go away. To help lessen these effects, sometimes the medication dose can be reduced, or the time of day it is taken can be changed.

- Agitation (feeling jittery).

- Sexual problems, which can affect both men and women. These include reduced sex drive and problems having and enjoying sex.

Some antidepressants are more likely to cause certain side effects than other types. Your doctor or pharmacist can answer questions about these medications. Any unusual reactions or side effects should be reported to a doctor immediately.

For the most up-to-date information on medications for treating bipolar disorder and their side effects, please see the online NIMH Medications booklet.

Should women who are pregnant or may become pregnant take medication for bipolar disorder?

Women with bipolar disorder who are pregnant or may become pregnant face special challenges. The mood stabilizing medications in use today can harm a developing fetus or nursing infant.39 But stopping medications, either suddenly or gradually, greatly increases the risk that bipolar symptoms will recur during pregnancy.40

Scientists are not sure yet, but lithium is likely the preferred mood-stabilizing medication for pregnant women with bipolar disorder.40, 41 However, lithium can lead to heart problems in the fetus. Women need to know that most bipolar medications are passed on through breast milk.41 Pregnant women and nursing mothers should talk to their doctors about the benefits and risks of all available treatments.

Psychotherapy

In addition to medication, psychotherapy, or "talk" therapy, can be an effective treatment for bipolar disorder. It can provide support, education, and guidance to people with bipolar disorder and their families. Some psychotherapy treatments used to treat bipolar disorder include:

1. Cognitive behavioral therapy (CBT) helps people with bipolar disorder learn to change harmful or negative thought patterns and behaviors.

2. Family-focused therapy includes family members. It helps enhance family coping strategies, such as recognizing new episodes early and helping their loved one. This therapy also improves communication and problem-solving.

3. Interpersonal and social rhythm therapy helps people with bipolar disorder improve their relationships with others and manage their daily routines. Regular daily routines and sleep schedules may help protect against manic episodes.

4. Psychoeducation teaches people with bipolar disorder about the illness and its treatment. This treatment helps people recognize signs of relapse so they can seek treatment early, before a full-blown episode occurs. Usually done in a group,

psychoeducation may also be helpful for family members and caregivers.

A licensed psychologist, social worker, or counselor typically provides these therapies. This mental health professional often works with the psychiatrist to track progress. The number, frequency, and type of sessions should be based on the treatment needs of each person. As with medication, following the doctor's instructions for any psychotherapy will provide the greatest benefit.

For more information, see the Substance Abuse and Mental Health Services Administration web page on choosing a mental health therapist.

Recently, NIMH funded a clinical trial called the Systematic Treatment Enhancement Program for Bipolar Disorder (STEP-BD). This was the largest treatment study ever conducted for bipolar disorder. In a study on psychotherapies, STEP-BD researchers compared people in two groups. The first group was treated with collaborative care (three sessions of psychoeducation over six weeks). The second group was treated with medication and intensive psychotherapy (30 sessions over nine months of CBT, interpersonal and social rhythm therapy, or family-focused therapy). Researchers found that the second group had fewer relapses, lower hospitalization rates, and were better able to stick with their treatment plans.42 They were also more likely to get well faster and stay well longer.

NIMH is supporting more research on which combinations of psychotherapy and medication work best. The goal is to help people with bipolar disorder live symptom-free for longer periods and to recover from episodes more quickly. Researchers also hope to determine whether psychotherapy helps delay the start of bipolar disorder in children at high risk for the illness.

Visit the NIMH Web site for more information on psychotherapy.

Other treatments

1. Electroconvulsive Therapy (ECT)—For cases in which medication and/or psychotherapy does not work, electroconvulsive therapy (ECT) may be useful. ECT, formerly known as "shock therapy," once had a bad reputation. But in recent years, it has greatly improved and can provide relief for people with severe bipolar disorder who have not been able to feel better with other treatments.

Before ECT is administered, a patient takes a muscle relaxant and is put under brief anesthesia. He or she does not consciously feel the electrical impulse administered in ECT. On average, ECT treatments last from 30–90 seconds. People who have ECT usually recover after 5–15 minutes and are able to go home the same day.43

Sometimes ECT is used for bipolar symptoms when other medical conditions, including pregnancy, make the use of medications too risky. ECT is a highly effective treatment for severely depressive, manic, or mixed episodes, but is generally not a first-line treatment.

ECT may cause some short-term side effects, including confusion, disorientation, and memory loss. But these side effects typically clear soon after treatment. People with bipolar disorder should discuss possible benefits and risks of ECT with an experienced doctor.44

2. Sleep Medications—People with bipolar disorder who have trouble sleeping usually sleep better after getting treatment for bipolar disorder. However, if sleeplessness does not improve, the doctor may suggest a change in medications. If the problems still continue, the doctor may prescribe sedatives or other sleep medications.

People with bipolar disorder should tell their doctor about all prescription drugs, over-the-counter medications, or supplements they are taking. Certain medications and supplements taken together may cause unwanted or dangerous effects.

Herbal Supplements

In general, there is not much research about herbal or natural supplements. Little is known about their effects on bipolar disorder. An herb called St. John's wort (Hypericum perforatum), often marketed as a natural antidepressant, may cause a switch to mania in some people with bipolar disorder.45 St. John's wort can also make other medications less effective, including some antidepressant and anticonvulsant medications.46 Scientists are also researching omega-3 fatty acids (most commonly found in fish oil) to measure their usefulness for long-term treatment of bipolar disorder.47 Study results have been mixed.48 It is important to talk with a doctor before taking any herbal or natural supplements because of the serious risk of interactions with other medications.

What can people with bipolar disorder expect from treatment?

Bipolar disorder has no cure, but can be effectively treated over the long-term. It is best controlled when treatment is continuous, rather than on and off. In the STEP-BD study, a little more than half of the people treated for bipolar disorder recovered over one year's time. For this study, recovery meant having two or fewer symptoms of the disorder for at least eight weeks.

However, even with proper treatment, mood changes can occur. In the STEP-BD study, almost half of those who recovered still had lingering symptoms. These people experienced a relapse or recurrence that was usually a return to a depressive state.49 If a person had a mental illness in addition to bipolar disorder, he or she was more likely to experience a relapse.49 Scientists are unsure, however, how these other illnesses or lingering symptoms increase the chance of relapse. For some people, combining psychotherapy with medication may help to prevent or delay relapse.42

Treatment may be more effective when people work closely with a doctor and talk openly about their concerns and choices. Keeping track of mood changes and symptoms with a daily life chart can help a doctor assess a person's response to treatments. Sometimes the doctor needs to change a treatment plan to make sure symptoms are controlled most effectively. A psychiatrist should guide any changes in type or dose of medication.

How can I help a friend or relative who has bipolar disorder?

If you know someone who has bipolar disorder, it affects you too. The first and most important thing you can do is help him or her get the right diagnosis and treatment. You may need to make the appointment and go with him or her to see the doctor. Encourage your loved one to stay in treatment.

To help a friend or relative, you can:

- Offer emotional support, understanding, patience, and encouragement
- Learn about bipolar disorder so you can understand what your friend or relative is experiencing

- Talk to your friend or relative and listen carefully

- Listen to feelings your friend or relative expresses-be understanding about situations that may trigger bipolar symptoms

- Invite your friend or relative out for positive distractions, such as walks, outings, and other activities

- Remind your friend or relative that, with time and treatment, he or she can get better.

Never ignore comments about your friend or relative harming himself or herself. Always report such comments to his or her therapist or doctor.

Support for caregivers

Like other serious illnesses, bipolar disorder can be difficult for spouses, family members, friends, and other caregivers. Relatives and friends often have to cope with the person's serious behavioral problems, such as wild spending sprees during mania, extreme withdrawal during depression, poor work or school performance. These behaviors can have lasting consequences.

Caregivers usually take care of the medical needs of their loved ones. The caregivers have to deal with how this affects their own health. The stress that caregivers are under may lead to missed work or lost free time, strained relationships with people who may not understand the situation, and physical and mental exhaustion.

Stress from caregiving can make it hard to cope with a loved one's bipolar symptoms. One study shows that if a caregiver is under a lot of stress, his or her loved one has more trouble following the treatment plan, which increases the chance for a major bipolar episode.50 It is important that people caring for those with bipolar disorder also take care of themselves.

How can I help myself if I have bipolar disorder?

It may be very hard to take that first step to help yourself. It may take time, but you can get better with treatment.

To help yourself:

- Talk to your doctor about treatment options and progress
- Keep a regular routine, such as eating meals at the same time every day and going to sleep at the same time every night
- Try to get enough sleep
- Stay on your medication
- Learn about warning signs signaling a shift into depression or mania

- Expect your symptoms to improve gradually, not immediately.

Where can I go for help?

If you are unsure where to go for help, ask your family doctor. Others who can help are listed below.

- Mental health specialists, such as psychiatrists, psychologists, social workers, or mental health counselors
- Health maintenance organizations
- Community mental health centers
- Hospital psychiatry departments and outpatient clinics
- Mental health programs at universities or medical schools
- State hospital outpatient clinics
- Family services, social agencies, or clergy

- Peer support groups
- Private clinics and facilities
- Employee assistance programs
- Local medical and/or psychiatric societies.

You can also check the phone book under "mental health," "health," "social services," "hotlines," or "physicians" for phone numbers and addresses. An emergency room doctor can also provide temporary help and can tell you where and how to get further help.

What if I or someone I know is in crisis?

If you are thinking about harming yourself, or know someone who is, tell someone who can help immediately.

* Call your doctor.

* Call 911 or go to a hospital emergency room to get immediate help or ask a friend or family member to help you do these things.

* Call the toll-free, 24-hour hotline of the National Suicide Prevention Lifeline at 1-800-273-TALK (1-800-273-8255); TTY: 1-800-799-4TTY (4889) to talk to a trained counselor.

Make sure you or the suicidal person is not left alone.

Citations

1. Kessler RC, Berglund P, Demler O, Jin R, Merikangas KR, Walters EE. Lifetime prevalence and age-of-onset distributions of DSM-IV disorders in the National Comorbidity Survey Replication. Arch Gen Psychiatry. 2005 Jun;62(6):593-602.

2. Akiskal HS. "Mood Disorders: Clinical Features." in Sadock BJ, Sadock VA (ed). (2005). Kaplan & Sadock's Comprehensive Textbook of Psychiatry. Lippincott Williams & Wilkins:Philadelphia.

3. Schneck CD, Miklowitz DJ, Miyahara S, Araga M, Wisniewski S, Gyulai L, Allen MH, Thase ME, Sachs GS. The prospective course of rapid-cycling bipolar disorder: findings from the STEP-BD. Am J Psychiatry. 2008 Mar;165(3):370-7; quiz 410.

4. Schneck CD, Miklowitz DJ, Calabrese JR, Allen MH, Thomas MR, Wisniewski SR, Miyahara S, Shelton MD, Ketter TA, Goldberg JF, Bowden CL, Sachs GS. Phenomenology of rapid-cycling bipolar disorder: data from the first 500 participants in the Systematic Treatment Enhancement Program. Am J Psychiatry. 2004 Oct;161(10):1902-1908.

5. Goodwin FK, Jamison KR. (2007) Manic-Depressive Illness: Bipolar Disorders and Recurrent Depression, Second Edition. Oxford University Press:New York.

6. Constituency Survey: Living With Bipolar Disorder: How Far Have We Really Come? National Depressive and Manic-Depressive Association. 2001.

7. Bizzarri JV, Sbrana A, Rucci P, Ravani L, Massei GJ, Gonnelli C, Spagnolli S, Doria MR, Raimondi F, Endicott J, Dell'Osso L, Cassano GB. The spectrum of substance abuse in bipolar disorder: reasons for use, sensation seeking and substance sensitivity. Bipolar Disord. 2007 May;9(3):213-220.

8. Mueser KT, Goodman LB, Trumbetta SL, Rosenberg SD, Osher C, Vidaver R, Auciello P, Foy DW. Trauma and posttraumatic stress disorder in severe mental illness. J Consult Clin Psychol. 1998 Jun;66(3):493-499.

9. Strakowski SM, Sax KW, McElroy SL, Keck PE, Jr., Hawkins JM, West SA. Course of psychiatric and substance abuse syndromes co-occurring with bipolar disorder after a first psychiatric hospitalization. J Consult Clin Psychol. 1998 Sep;59(9):465-471.

10. Krishnan KR. Psychiatric and medical comorbidities of bipolar disorder. Psychosom Med. 2005 Jan-Feb;67(1):1-8.

11. Kupfer DJ. The increasing medical burden in bipolar disorder. JAMA. 2005 May 25;293(20):2528-2530.

12. Nurnberger JI, Jr., Foroud T. Genetics of bipolar affective disorder. Curr Psychiatry Rep. 2000 Apr;2(2):147-157.

13. Potash JB, Toolan J, Steele J, Miller EB, Pearl J, Zandi PP, Schulze TG, Kassem L, Simpson SG, Lopez V, MacKinnon DF, McMahon FJ. The bipolar disorder phenome database: a resource for genetic studies. Am J Psychiatry. 2007 Aug;164(8):1229-1237.

14. Soares JC, Mann JJ. The functional neuroanatomy of mood disorders. J Psychiatr Res. 1997 Jul-Aug;31(4):393-432.

15. Soares JC, Mann JJ. The anatomy of mood disorders--review of structural neuroimaging studies. Biol Psychiatry. 1997 Jan 1;41(1):86-106.

16. Gogtay N, Ordonez A, Herman DH, Hayashi KM, Greenstein D, Vaituzis C, Lenane M, Clasen L, Sharp W, Giedd JN, Jung D, Nugent Iii TF, Toga AW, Leibenluft E, Thompson PM, Rapoport JL. Dynamic mapping of cortical development

before and after the onset of pediatric bipolar illness. J Child Psychol Psychiatry. 2007 Sep;48(9):852-862.

17. Hirschfeld RM. Psychiatric Management, from "Guideline Watch: Practice Guideline for the Treatment of Patients With Bipolar Disorder, 2nd Edition". http://www.psychiatryonline.com/content.aspx?aID=148440. Accessed on February 11, 2008.

18. Sachs GS, Printz DJ, Kahn DA, Carpenter D, Docherty JP. The Expert Consensus Guideline Series: Medication Treatment of Bipolar Disorder 2000. Postgrad Med. 2000 Apr;Spec No.:1-104.

19. Sachs GS, Thase ME. Bipolar disorder therapeutics: maintenance treatment. Biol Psychiatry. 2000 Sep 15;48(6):573-581.

20. Huxley NA, Parikh SV, Baldessarini RJ. Effectiveness of psychosocial treatments in bipolar disorder: state of the evidence. Harv Rev Psychiatry. 2000 Sep;8(3):126-140.

21. Miklowitz DJ. A review of evidence-based psychosocial interventions for bipolar disorder. J Consult Clin Psychol. 2006 67(Suppl 11):28-33.

22. Kupka RW, Nolen WA, Post RM, McElroy SL, Altshuler LL, Denicoff KD, Frye MA, Keck PE, Jr., Leverich GS, Rush AJ, Suppes T, Pollio C, Drexhage HA. High rate of autoimmune thyroiditis in bipolar disorder: lack of association with lithium exposure. Biol Psychiatry. 2002 Feb 15;51(4):305-311.

23. Bowden CL, Calabrese JR, McElroy SL, Gyulai L, Wassef A, Petty F, Pope HG, Jr., Chou JC, Keck PE, Jr., Rhodes LJ, Swann AC, Hirschfeld RM, Wozniak PJ, Group DMS. A randomized, placebo-controlled 12-month trial of divalproex and lithium in treatment of outpatients with bipolar I disorder. Arch Gen Psychiatry. 2000 May;57(5):481-489.

24. Calabrese JR, Shelton MD, Rapport DJ, Youngstrom EA, Jackson K, Bilali S, Ganocy SJ, Findling RL. A 20-month, double-blind, maintenance trial of lithium versus divalproex in rapid-cycling bipolar disorder. Am J Psychiatry. 2005 Nov;162(11):2152-2161.

25. Vainionpaa LK, Rattya J, Knip M, Tapanainen JS, Pakarinen AJ, Lanning P, Tekay A, Myllyla VV, Isojarvi JI. Valproate-induced hyperandrogenism during pubertal maturation in girls with epilepsy. Ann Neurol. 1999 Apr;45(4):444-450.

26. Joffe H, Cohen LS, Suppes T, McLaughlin WL, Lavori P, Adams JM, Hwang CH, Hall JE, Sachs GS. Valproate is associated with new-onset oligoamenorrhea with hyperandrogenism in women with bipolar disorder. Biol Psychiatry. 2006 Jun 1;59(11):1078-1086.

27. Joffe H, Cohen LS, Suppes T, Hwang CH, Molay F, Adams JM, Sachs GS, Hall JE. Longitudinal follow-up of reproductive and metabolic features of valproate-associated polycystic ovarian syndrome features: A preliminary report. Biol Psychiatry. 2006 Dec 15;60(12):1378-1381.

28. Tohen M, Sanger TM, McElroy SL, Tollefson GD, Chengappa KN, Daniel DG, Petty F, Centorrino F, Wang R, Grundy SL, Greaney MG, Jacobs TG, David SR, Toma V. Olanzapine versus placebo in the treatment of acute mania. Olanzapine HGEH Study Group. Am J Psychiatry. 1999 May;156(5):702-709.

29. Thase ME, Sachs GS. Bipolar depression: pharmacotherapy and related therapeutic strategies. Biol Psychiatry. 2000 Sep 15;48(6):558-572.

30. Sachs GS, Nierenberg AA, Calabrese JR, Marangell LB, Wisniewski SR, Gyulai L, Friedman ES, Bowden CL, Fossey MD, Ostacher MJ, Ketter TA, Patel J, Hauser P, Rapport D, Martinez JM, Allen MH, Miklowitz DJ, Otto MW,

Dennehy EB, Thase ME. Effectiveness of adjunctive antidepressant treatment for bipolar depression. N Engl J Med. 2007 Apr 26;356(17):1711-1722.

31. MedlinePlus Drug Information: Lithium. http://www.nlm.nih.gov/medlineplus/druginfo/medmaster/a681039.html. Accessed on Nov 19, 2007.

32. MedlinePlus Drug Information: Carbamazepine. http://www.nlm.nih.gov/medlineplus/druginfo/medmaster/a682237.html. Accessed on July 13, 2007.

33. MedlinePlus Drug Information: Lamotrigine. http://www.nlm.nih.gov/medlineplus/druginfo/medmaster/a695007.html. Accessed on February 12, 2008.

34. MedlinePlus Drug Information: Valproic Acid. http://www.nlm.nih.gov/medlineplus/druginfo/medmaster/a682412.html. Accessed on February 12, 2008.

35. MedlinePlus Drug Information: Topiramate. http://www.nlm.nih.gov/medlineplus/druginfo/medmaster/a697012.html. Accessed on Febrary 22, 2008.

36. MedlinePlus Drug Information: Gabapentin. http://www.nlm.nih.gov/medlineplus/druginfo/medmaster/a694007.html. Accessed on February 22, 2008.

37. MedlinePlus Drug Information: Oxcarbazepine. http://www.nlm.nih.gov/medlineplus/druginfo/medmaster/a601245.html. Accessed on February 22, 2008.

38. Lieberman JA, Stroup TS, McEvoy JP, Swartz MS, Rosenheck RA, Perkins DO, Keefe RS, Davis SM, Davis CE, Lebowitz BD, Severe J, Hsiao JK. Effectiveness of antipsychotic drugs in patients with chronic schizophrenia. N Engl J Med. 2005 Sep 22;353(12):1209-1223.

39. Llewellyn A, Stowe ZN, Strader JR, Jr. The use of lithium and management of women with bipolar disorder during pregnancy and lactation. J Consult Clin Psychol. 1998 59(Suppl 6):57-64.

40. Viguera AC, Whitfield T, Baldessarini RJ, Newport J, Stowe Z, Reminick A, Zurick A, Cohen LS. Risk of recurrence in women with bipolar disorder during pregnancy: prospective study of mood stabilizer discontinuation. Am J Psychiatry. 2007 Dec;164(12):1817-1824.

41. Yonkers KA, Wisner KL, Stowe Z, Leibenluft E, Cohen L, Miller L, Manber R, Viguera A, Suppes T, Altshuler L. Management of bipolar disorder during pregnancy and the postpartum period. Am J Psychiatry. 2004 Apr;161(4):608-620.

42. Miklowitz DJ, Otto MW, Frank E, Reilly-Harrington NA, Wisniewski SR, Kogan JN, Nierenberg AA, Calabrese JR, Marangell LB, Gyulai L, Araga M, Gonzalez JM, Shirley ER, Thase ME, Sachs GS. Psychosocial treatments for bipolar depression: a 1-year randomized trial from the Systematic Treatment Enhancement Program (STEP). Arch Gen Psychiatry. 2007 Apr;64(4):419-426.

43. Pandya M, Pozuelo L, Malone D. Electroconvulsive therapy: what the internist needs to know. Cleve Clin J Med. 2007 Sep;74(9):679-685.

44. Mental Health: A Report of the Surgeon General. U.S. Department of Health and Human Services, Substance Abuse and Mental Health Services Administration, Center for Mental Health Services, National Institutes of Health, National Institute of Mental Health. 1999.

45. Nierenberg AA, Burt T, Matthews J, Weiss AP. Mania associated with St. John's wort. Biol Psychiatry. 1999 Dec 15;46(12):1707-1708.

46. Henney JE. From the Food and Drug Administration: Risk of Drug Interactions With St John's Wort. JAMA. 2000 Apr 5;283(13):1679.

47. Stoll AL, Severus WE, Freeman MP, Rueter S, Zboyan HA, Diamond E, Cress KK, Marangell LB. Omega 3 fatty acids in bipolar disorder: a preliminary double-blind, placebo-controlled trial. Arch Gen Psychiatry. 1999 May;56(5):407-412.

48. Freeman MP, Hibbeln JR, Wisner KL, Davis JM, Mischoulon D, Peet M, Keck PE, Jr., Marangell LB, Richardson AJ, Lake J, Stoll AL. Omega-3 fatty acids: evidence basis for treatment and future research in psychiatry. J Consult Clin Psychol. 2006 Dec;67(12):1954-1967.

49. Perlis RH, Ostacher MJ, Patel JK, Marangell LB, Zhang H, Wisniewski SR, Ketter TA, Miklowitz DJ, Otto MW, Gyulai L, Reilly-Harrington NA, Nierenberg AA, Sachs GS, Thase ME. Predictors of recurrence in bipolar disorder: primary outcomes from the Systematic Treatment Enhancement Program for Bipolar Disorder (STEP-BD). Am J Psychiatry. 2006 Feb;163(2):217-224.

50. Perlick DA, Rosenheck RA, Clarkin JF, Maciejewski PK, Sirey J, Struening E, Link BG. Impact of family burden and affective response on clinical outcome among patients with bipolar disorder. Psychiatr Serv. 2004 Sep;55(9):1029-1035.

For more information on bipolar disorder

Visit the National Library of Medicine's MedlinePlus, and En Español

For information on NIMH supported clinical trials, the Clinical trials at NIMH in Bethesda, MD or visit the National Library of Medicine Clinical Trials Database

Information from NIMH is available in multiple formats. You can browse online, download documents in PDF, and order materials through the mail. Check the NIMH Web site for the latest information on this topic and to order publications.

If you do not have Internet access please contact the NIMH Information Center at the numbers listed below.

National Institute of Mental Health

Science Writing, Press & Dissemination Branch

6001 Executive Boulevard

Room 8184, MSC 9663

Bethesda, MD 20892-9663

Phone: 301-443-4513 or

1-866-615-NIMH (6464) toll-free

TTY: 301-443-8431

TTY: 866-415-8051 toll-free

FAX: 301-443-4279

E-mail: nimhinfo@nih.gov

Web site: http://www.nimh.nih.gov